This journal belongs to:

_____

_____

_____

_____

This journal is designed to be used with The Pre-Marriage Course sessions.
Please see page 93 for more information on how to join or run a course.

The Pre-Marriage Course Journal
© 2001, 2020 by Alpha International

Published in Grand Rapids, Michigan, by HarperChristian Resources. HarperChristian Resources is a registered trademark of The Zondervan Corporation, L.L.C., a wholly owned subsidary of HarperCollins Christian Publishing, Inc.

Requests for information should be addressed to customercare@harpercollins.com.

ISBN 9780310122500 (softcover)
ISBN 9780310122449 (ebook)

The Alpha name and trademarks are used under license from Alpha International.
Alpha USA, PO Box 7491, Carol Stream, IL 60197-7491

HarperChristian Resources titles may be purchased in bulk for church, business, fundraising, or ministry use. For information, please e-mail ResourceSpecialist@ChurchSource.com.

Printed in the United States of America

24 25 26 27 28 LBC 8 7 6 5 4

Contents

How to use this journal

To help you get the most out of your journal, we have used symbols for specific activities:

 When you write something down

 When you talk with your partner

 When you sit back and reflect

 When you note down your intentions—for example, your plans for a date night or hopes for the future

 When you swap journals and write something in your partner's journal that will be helpful for them to look back on in the future

Following the course, we hope the journal will serve as a reminder of what you've discovered about each other and the journey you're on as a couple, and help you to put into practice what you've learned.

Welcome to The Pre-Marriage Course. . .

This course is built on universal principles about marriage that are relevant to any couple, anywhere.

Strong marriages don't just develop automatically. Our hope is that you'll discover the attitudes, the values, and the habits that are needed to build a healthy and strong marriage that will last a lifetime.

This journal is designed for you to be able to reflect, to talk, and to dream together about your future, not only on the course but afterwards too. There are no right or wrong answers and no one else will see your journal.

Our hope is that you will pick up tools from the course that you can use to invest in your marriage for the rest of your lives. And we hope you'll have fun finding out things you didn't previously know about your partner.

Whether you are engaged or exploring marriage, you are on an exciting journey.

Nicky and Sila

Nicky and Sila Lee
Creators of The Pre-Marriage Course

Communication

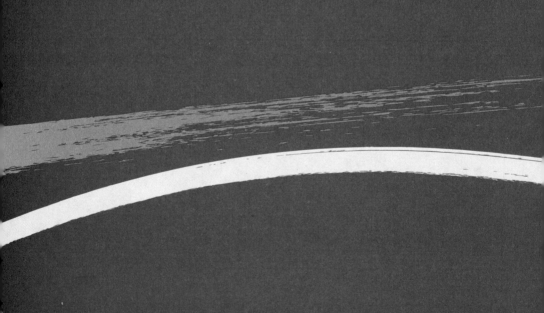

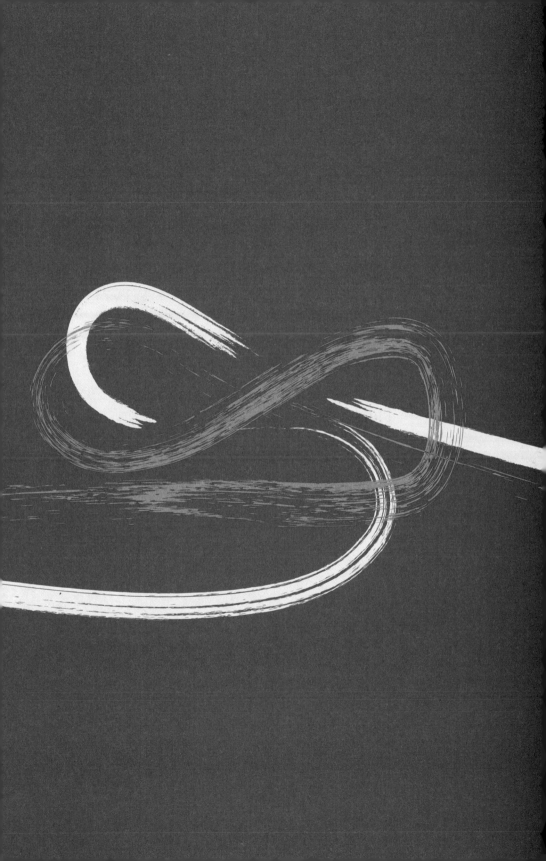

Session 1 – Communication

> "
>
> **Marriage is a commitment that says, "I'm prepared, not only to spend the rest of my life with you, but to spend the rest of my life finding out about you. There's always going to be more of you to discover."**
>
> DR. ROWAN WILLIAMS (FORMER ARCHBISHOP OF CANTERBURY)

It's only when we get married that we realize that some of our deeply held assumptions about life are not universally shared!

CONVERSATION 1

5 minutes

DIFFERENT EXPECTATIONS

See if you can each identify one difference in your expectations for marriage that you have as a result of your family upbringing or your different cultural backgrounds.

For example: *level of involvement with your wider family; how often you invite visitors to your home; whether you have new or old furniture; whether you throw broken things away or mend them; who does most of the cooking; how you relax.*

Learning to communicate

Communication involves talking and listening effectively.

We are all different in the way we communicate and this is affected by:

- **- our personality**

- **- our background**

1. Our personality

Extrovert
They tend towards processing their thoughts externally. In other words, they tend to think out loud.

Introvert
They tend towards organizing their thoughts in their heads first before they speak.

Analytical
They work things out methodically and may take a long time to make decisions.

Intuitive
They often act on hunches and may jump to conclusions.

> **Being able to talk openly and honestly about our differences is vital if we're to have a strong marriage.**

"I will praise You, because I have been remarkably and wondrously made."
— PSALM 139:14, CSB

HOW WE COMMUNICATE

Tell your partner how you think their personality affects the way they communicate.

2. Our family background

Some families are quiet, others are much louder.

Some families are more volatile, others are calmer.

Some families take turns to talk, others frequently interrupt.

Some families air differences immediately; others may delay or avoid talking about conflicting views at all.

CONVERSATION 3

10 minutes

FAMILY STYLES OF COMMUNICATION

Complete the following exercise on your own and then talk about it together.
Mark with an "x" where you think your own family comes on the line between
the two extremes.

Overall, the communication in my family was:

Indirect ├──┤ Direct

Vague ├──┤ Specific

Relaxed ├──┤ Stressful

Non-confrontational ├─────────────────────────────────┤ Confrontational

Closed ├───┤ Open

Loud ├───┤ Quiet

Humorous ├──┤ Serious

Interrupting ├──┤ Taking turns

How has the way your family communicated when you were growing up affected the
way you communicate now as an adult? How different is this to the way your partner's
family communicates?

Hindrances to good communication

1. Failing to make time

Set aside time for meaningful conversation on a regular basis.

- plan this time (it doesn't just happen)
- guard this time from distractions and interruptions, such as phones and other screens

Recognize when to drop everything and listen.

What could be the things that prevent you from having time to talk together daily?

2. Failing to talk about our feelings

Some people have to learn how to talk about their feelings as they may have had no role model growing up

- they may find talking about their feelings difficult because of inadequacy, vulnerability, or fear of how the other person will respond
- dare to trust your partner with your feelings

Listen to each other without judging or criticizing.

CONVERSATION 4

10 minutes

EFFECTIVE TALKING

– Take turns to tell each other how you tend to communicate when you're feeling anxious, irritated, or under pressure.

– Are you imitating what you observed growing up?

– Ask your partner how difficult or easy it is for them to talk about their inner thoughts, attitudes, and emotions.

– Find out if they were encouraged to talk about their feelings during their upbringing.

Sharing our innermost thoughts and feelings is essential for building a strong marriage.

3. Failing to listen to each other

> Listening is of huge importance for building a foundation of understanding and intimacy in marriage.

Not being listened to is highly damaging to a relationship.

When someone listens to us, we feel:

- understood
- valued
- supported
- loved

Overcome **bad listening habits** such as:

- disengaging
- going off on a tangent
- giving advice
- reassuring
- interrupting

Do you recognize any of these bad listening habits in yourself?

How to listen

It takes patience to learn how to listen effectively.

Listening effectively means:

- allowing our partner to finish what they want to say

- putting aside our own agenda and seeking to see the world through our partner's eyes

- making the effort to understand them when they think or feel differently to us

CONVERSATION 5

15 minutes

EFFECTIVE LISTENING

1. One of you say to your partner, **"Tell me about something that is worrying you."**

   Listen carefully and, when they have finished, reflect back what they have said, particularly about their feelings, to show that you have understood.
   If you did not understand, ask your partner to tell you again.

2. Then ask, **"What's concerning you most about what you've told me?"** Reflect back what they have said.

3. Then ask, **"Is there anything you could do (or, if appropriate, you'd like me or us to do) about what you've just said?"** Again, reflect back to them what they say.

4. Finally ask, **"Is there anything else you would like to say?"** Reflect back what they have said.

Then swap roles.

Continuing the Conversation

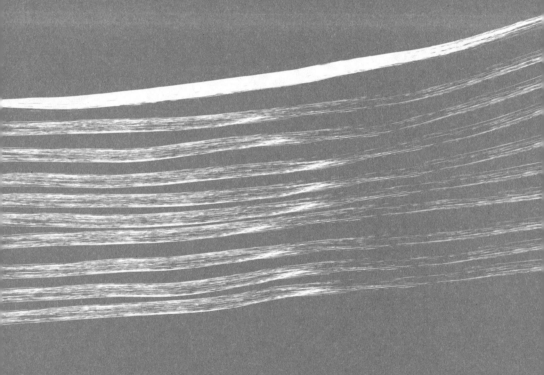

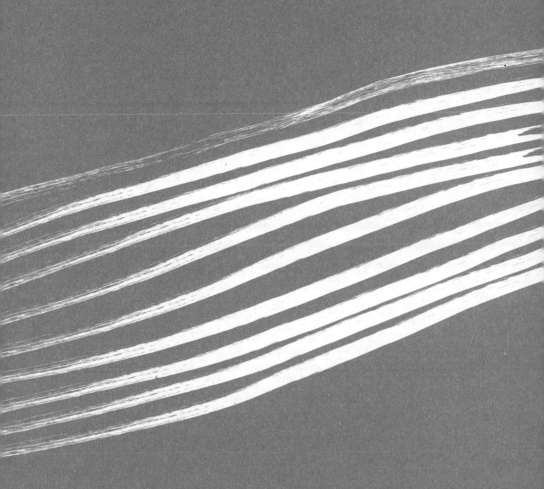

"The gift of being a good listener, a gift which requires constant practice, is perhaps the most healing gift anyone could possess. It doesn't judge or advise the other, but communicates support at a level deeper than words."

— Gerard Hughes

Plan a date together

	Mon	Tues	Wed	Thurs	Fri	Sat	Sun
☀️ Morning							
☁️ Afternoon							
🌙 Evening							

My turn / your turn to organize what we do.

This week, we could...

Conversation starter on our next date

Ask your partner, "What is the best vacation you have ever been on?"

And, "Where would your dream vacation destination be?"

What are you hoping to gain from the course?

Effective communication

Take some time over the next week to write down your answers
to the following questions and then discuss them with your partner.

1. Are you a good listener?

On a rating of 1 to 10 score your ability as a listener:

1 2 3 4 5 6 7 8 9 10

2. How would you rate your partner?

1 2 3 4 5 6 7 8 9 10

3. When have you had the best conversations about your deepest thoughts and emotions?

4. Which times and places are most conducive to good communication?

5. What have been the worst times and places for communicating effectively? Can you work out why?

6. Complete the following: I find it easier to be open and vulnerable with you when you…

This exercise is adapted from *Looking up the Aisle* by Dave and Joyce Ames
(*Mission to Marriage*, 1994).

Session 2

Conflict

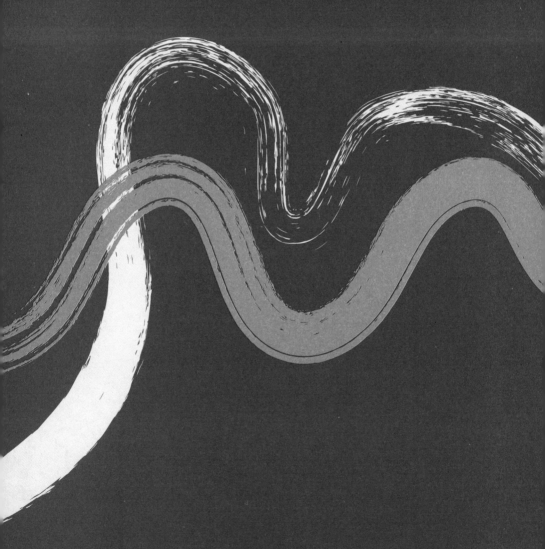

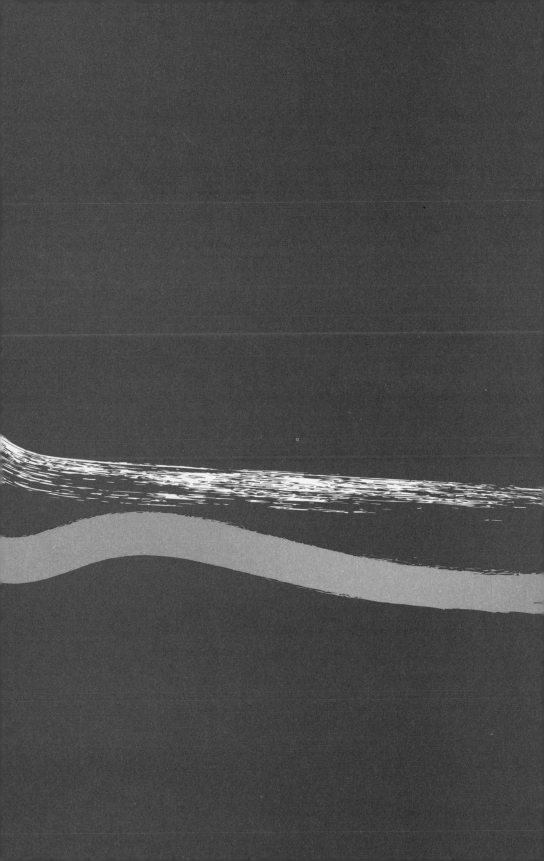

RECAP

– Tell each other something new that you learned about marriage on Session 1 and something new you learned about your partner.

– Then tell each other what it felt like to be listened to in Session 1, Conversation 5, "Effective Listening" (on page 15).

Session 2 – Conflict

Expecting conflict

Conflict is inevitable in every relationship

- we're different - with different backgrounds, different desires, different priorities, different personalities

- we're all naturally self-centered to some degree

> The issue isn't whether we'll disagree; the issue is how we deal with those disagreements. The really important thing for every couple is to have the tools to resolve conflict constructively.

Managing anger

Anger is not wrong in itself; it is how we manage our anger that can be damaging.

Two animals help to illustrate two inappropriate and unhelpful ways of managing our anger:

- **rhinos:** let you know they're angry right away—they go on the attack

- **hedgehogs:** tend to hide their anger—they're likely to become quiet and withdraw

- both are damaging and ineffective ways of resolving conflict

Rhinos and hedgehogs can learn to air disagreements in a constructive way without hurting each other in the process.

CONVERSATION 1

10 minutes

RHINOS AND HEDGEHOGS

Ask yourself if you have more rhino or more hedgehog tendencies when you are angry. If you are not sure, check with your partner who may have a better idea!

Talk about how each of you typically responds when you feel hurt and how you display anger.

Recognizing and accepting our differences

Some of our differences have to do with our personality:

- more cautious / more impulsive

- organized / go with the flow

- take charge / prefer to support

- more extroverted / more introverted

- like to save money / like spending money

One personality preference isn't better or worse than the other—it's just different.

We can't expect our partner to change to be like us.

> By recognizing and accepting our differences, we can learn to appreciate each other's strengths and support each other's weaknesses. In that way, we can work together effectively as a team.

CONVERSATION 2

10 minutes

RECOGNIZING YOUR DIFFERENCES

1. Mark against each issue where on the line your partner's and your own preferences each lie, *e.g., N = Nicky; S = Sila*

Money	S	N
	Spend	Save

Punctuality	S	N
	Arrive early	Nearly late

ISSUE	PREFERENCE	
Money	Spend	Save
Holidays	Adventure	Rest
People	Spend time with others	Spend time alone
Sleeping	Go to bed late	Get up early
Tidiness	Keep everything tidy/under control	Be relaxed/live in a mess
Disagreements	Pick a fight	Keep the peace
TV	Keep it on	Throw it out
Relaxation	Go out	Be at home
Punctuality	Arrive early	Nearly late
Planning	Make plans/stick to them	Be flexible/change plans
Organization	Organized	Disorganized
Decisions	Impulsive	Cautious
Family	See often	See rarely
Friends	Long list	A few close ones
Music	Like it on constantly	Only at certain times
Talking	Talkative	Quiet
Change	Enjoy change	Resist change
Initiative	Like to initiate	Prefer to respond to others' ideas
Focus	Goal focused	Relationship focused

2. Discuss how your differences can be complementary in your relationship.

Looking for solutions together

See that you're on the same side.

Look for an "us" solution.

Be ready to press the "pause button"

    - is this the right time?

    - is this the right place?

 The 10 o'clock rule

The 10 o'clock rule can be called into play by either you or your partner if you are having an argument late in the evening. It means the argument has to be paused and postponed until a better time.

> **Looking for a solution together requires a shift of thinking to see that we're on the same side, not opposite sides, then discussing the issue together and looking for a solution that works for us.**

Five steps to finding a solution

1. Identify and focus on the issue causing conflict

Take the issue that is causing conflict from between you.

Put it out in front of you and work on it together.

2. Use "I" statements

Avoid labeling—for example: *"You always…" / "You never…"*

Describe your feelings—for example: *"I feel upset by…"*

3. Listen to each other

Try to understand and value each other's perspective.

Take turns to talk.

4. Brainstorm possible solutions

Talk about different possibilities.

It may help to write a list.

5. Choose the best solution for now and review later

If it doesn't work, try another solution.

If you can't find a solution together, ask for help.

CONVERSATION 3

10 minutes

USING THE FIVE STEPS

1. What patterns of resolving, or failing to resolve, conflict did you observe in your parents' (or main caregivers') marriage?

2. What are the trigger points for conflict in your relationship?

3. What causes conflict to escalate and what helps each of you to hit the "pause button"?

4. Which is the most important of the five steps for resolving conflict for each of you?

Process for healing hurt

Hurt is inevitable in marriage and this hurt must be healed if our relationship is to flourish.

There is a simple but powerful process for healing:

1. Talk about the hurt

Tell your partner when they have upset you.

Don't hold on to hurt or allow self-pity and resentment to build up.

> Try asking each other regularly, "Is there anything you need to forgive me for?"

2. Say sorry

Pride can make it hard to say sorry.

Apologizing means taking responsibility for our wrong words or actions.

Do you find it hard to tell your partner when they have upset you or to say sorry when you have hurt them?

3. Forgive

Forgiveness is the greatest force for healing in a marriage.

Forgiveness IS NOT:

- forgetting the hurt happened

- pretending it doesn't matter

- failing to confront our partner's wrong and hurtful behavior

---

"*[Love] keeps no record of wrongs.*"

— 1 CORINTHIANS 13:5

Forgiveness IS:

- facing the wrong done to us

- recognizing the emotions inside

- choosing not to hold the offence against our partner

- giving up our self-pity

Forgiveness is first and foremost a choice, not a feeling

- new feelings follow forgiveness

- forgiveness is a process—we often need to keep on forgiving (sometimes on a daily basis)

- forgiveness deals with anger and resentment—although we might still feel hurt until healing is complete

> "
>
> The word resentment expresses what happens if the cycle of blame goes uninterrupted. It means literally, "to feel again"; resentment clings to the past, relives it over and over, picks each fresh scab so that the wound never heals.
>
> *WHAT'S SO AMAZING ABOUT GRACE?* BY PHILIP YANCEY

"Bear with each other and forgive whatever grievances you may have against one another. Forgive as the Lord forgave you."

— COLOSSIANS 3:13

CONVERSATION 4

15 minutes

HEALING HURT

Fill in points 1 and 2 with anything that comes to mind.

1. I feel hurt by what you did / didn't do / said / didn't say when:

2. I think you may be carrying hurt by what I did / didn't do / said / didn't say when:

Show each other and reflect back what your partner has written. Then amend point 2 if necessary. Now, or later, complete points 3 and 4.

3. I am so sorry for:

4. I choose to forgive you for:

Take turns to say to your partner what you have written for points 3 and 4. If necessary, take more time over the coming week to resolve these issues. If you get stuck as a couple, ask for help.

Continuing the Conversation

"Identifying and focussing on the issue is often the most important part of preventing conflicts escalating."

— Nicky and Sila Lee

Plan a date together

	Mon	Tue	Wed	Thur	Fri	Sat	Sun
☀ Morning							
☁ Afternoon							
🌙 Evening							

My turn / your turn to organize what we do.

This week, we could...

Conversation starter on our next date

Ask your partner, "What makes us both laugh?"

And, "What could we do to create more times of fun and laughter between us?"

What does forgiveness mean to you?

How easy do you find it to forgive?

Think back to your upbringing: can you identify the people in your family who reacted more as the rhino and those who reacted more as the hedgehog in an argument?

Finding agreement

Agree on a suitable time and place to discuss one important issue that is causing disagreement between you.

1. Identify the issue.

2. How have each of you responded to this issue in the past?

Me

You

3. Both write down what you consider the main concern you each have regarding the issue.

Me

You

Discuss what you have each written down. Take turns to talk and be sure to listen to each other's point of view without blaming or criticizing.

4. Brainstorm possible solutions—do not rule out any at this stage.

1.

2.

3.

4.

5. Discuss the solutions to see which one would work best.

6. Try that solution. If it doesn't seem to work, go back to your list and try another one.

Commitment

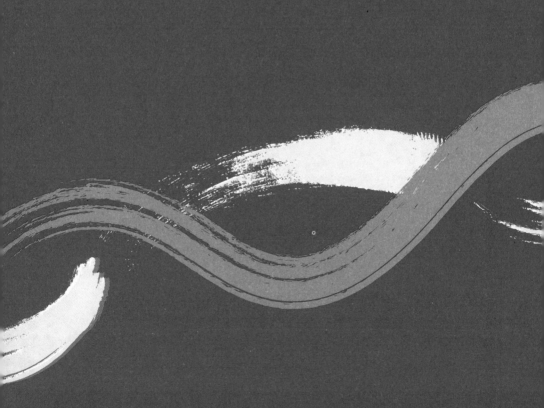

RECAP

– Look back at Session 2 to remind yourself what was covered.

– Then discuss with your partner which of your differences cause conflict and how these could be complementary in your relationship.

Session 3 – Commitment

> Making a commitment to each other enables us to plan our future together; it allows us to try things out, to get things wrong, to forgive, to have the confidence to raise issues, and to make ourselves vulnerable—commitment is "the essence of marriage", its very heart.

Two consequences of commitment in marriage:

1. Friendship

Marriage meets our longing for connection, for intimacy.

Marriage isn't the only way to counter aloneness but it is the closest possible human relationship.

"It is not good for the man to be alone."
— GENESIS 2:18

"This is now bone of my bones and flesh of my flesh."
— GENESIS 2:23

2. Family life

The ideal is for children to grow up seeing an intimate, committed, long-term relationship between their parents.

One of the best ways parents can love their children is by loving each other.

A strong marriage can break a cycle of failed relationships.

>
> " "
>
> **There is no perfect marriage. There are bound to be arguments or disagreements but what matters is coming back together again and forgiving and loving each other. It's important that children learn that it's okay to have differing opinions.**
> DR. MOSUN DORGU

CONVERSATION 1

5 minutes

THE BENEFITS OF MARRIAGE

Discuss between the two of you:

- What, in your view, is the role of marriage in society?

- What excites you, or frightens you, about marriage?

"For this reason a man [and a woman] will leave their father and mother and be joined to [each other] and the two will become one flesh."

— GENESIS 2:24

Creating an equal partnership

Every couple has to work out:

    - who does what

    - who decides what

    - who takes the lead on those things that need to be done

We may hold assumptions from our parents' (or main role models') marriage.

Talk about your expectations.

What assumptions do you hold from your parents' (or main role models) marriage?

"Submit to one another out of reverence for Christ."

— EPHESIANS 5:21

Submitting to each other

New Testament model

- radical new way of living together

- requires mutual giving to each other (see Appendix 2)

- undermined male dominance

> Christian teaching has led to the marriage relationship coming to be seen as an equal partnership of mutual giving.

Submitting doesn't mean being passive

- opposite of demanding or controlling

- seeking to put each other first

- putting each other's needs before our own

Discover which responsibilities you are each best suited to

- use your differences to serve each other

- in some areas, take the lead and initiate

- in others, support your partner

Loving like this is very active and involves making sacrifices for the sake of the other.

> Submitting to one another is the key to a loving marriage

"Husbands, love your wives, just as Christ loved the church and gave himself up for her."
— EPHESIANS 5:25

CONVERSATION 2

10 minutes

DIVIDING RESPONSIBILITIES

1. Each write down up to to six areas for which you expect to take responsibility.

For example: *housework, cleaning the bathroom, taking out rubbish, cooking, paying bills, organizing vacations, ironing, thank you letters, driving, map-reading, DIY, earning money, gardening, insurance, shopping...*

1.   4.

2.   5.

3.   6.

2. Each write down up to six areas for which you expect your partner to take responsibility.

1.   4.

2.   5.

3.   6.

3. Each write down up to six areas that you expect will be a joint responsibility.

1.   4.

2.   5.

3.   6.

4. When you have finished, compare lists.

5. In which of these areas would you expect your partner to take the lead in marriage?

The marriage covenant

The covenant we make when we get married is a decision to give ourselves completely to each other in love, and is then a decision we reinforce day-by-day.

> **The marriage covenant holds a couple together when they go through tough times, as every couple will.**

The marriage vows bring deep security and provide us with a safe space

- within which we are able to be open and vulnerable with each other

- they give us the confidence to allow our partner to know us as we are (including revealing those parts we keep well hidden) and that builds intimacy

- the vows focus not on what our partner can do for us but on what we can do for them

Try asking your partner each day, "How can I make your day better?"

CONVERSATION 3

10 minutes

THE MARRIAGE VOWS

Read through the marriage vows together and decide which is the most important phrase for each of you. Explain your choice to your partner (see Appendix 3).

"Love and faithfulness meet together."

— PSALM 85:10

Dealing with finances

Marriage involves sharing everything.

Every couple needs to set aside time to discuss finances.

Recognize your different attitudes to money.

- are you more of a "saver" or a "spender"?

Make a budget together
(see Appendix 4, Creating a Budget)

- calculate your joint income

- calculate / forecast your expenses

- discuss the balance of spending / saving / giving

If you're in debt or you're aware that your spending is out of control, seek help.

Compare your feelings about money; ask yourself:

- does money fascinate me or bore me?

- does it make me feel anxious or confident?

- or excited or guilty?

- or out of control?

The aim in marriage is to develop a dynamic partnership in which we double the experience and wisdom we bring to managing our finances and work on them together as a team.

CONVERSATION 4

10 minutes

DISCUSSING YOUR FINANCES

Each of you fill in your answers to the following questions and then discuss what you have put.

1. Describe your attitude to shopping (check appropriate boxes):

☐ source of pleasure   ☐ like buying presents

☐ enjoy window shopping   ☐ occasionally use it as escapism

☐ impulsive and sometimes wasteful   ☐ only buy essentials

☐ only enjoy spending money on...   ☐ avoid whenever possible

2. Do you worry about running out of money?   yes   no

3. Will you have a joint bank account?   yes   no

4. Will you keep separate accounts?   yes   no

5. How will you balance spending, saving, and giving away?

6. Will you work out a budget?   yes   no

7. Can you keep control with a credit card?   yes   no

8. Are you in debt?   yes   no

   If so, by how much?

   Discuss your plans for repayment.

9. How much could each of you spend without consulting the other?

10. Who will manage your finances?

jointly   husband   wife

Managing relationships
with the wider family

1. Leaving

When we get married, our relationship with our parents must be different to the way it was as we were growing up

- our marriage takes priority

- our first loyalty is now to our husband or wife

We mustn't underestimate what a massive change this is, particularly if there is ongoing emotional dependence by one of us on a parent or the other way round.

Our marriage relationship becomes our new center of gravity

- the first place we look to for comfort, security, affection

- a new decision-making structure

> Make your own decisions and support each other, however small the issue may seem.

2. Respecting our parents

Prioritizing our marriage doesn't mean we stop loving or respecting our parents.

We put in boundaries, where necessary, as kindly and sensitively as we can.

Show gratitude to your parents for all they do and have done for you.

Stay in touch with them

- take the initiative

- decide together on level of contact with your parents and parents-in-law

CONVERSATION 5

10 minutes

PARENTS AND IN-LAWS

Discuss as a couple:

From the following list, what possible areas of tension can you foresee with your parent(s)/parent(s)-in-law?

1. Vacations

2. Christmas / other holidays

3. Finances

4. Interference

5. Frequency of visits

6. Length of phone calls

7. Changed loyalty

8. Other. . .

How could they be resolved?

> Our aim in marriage is to build mutually supportive relationships with our parents and our parents-in-law, rather than sidelining them or being controlled by them.

Continuing the Conversation

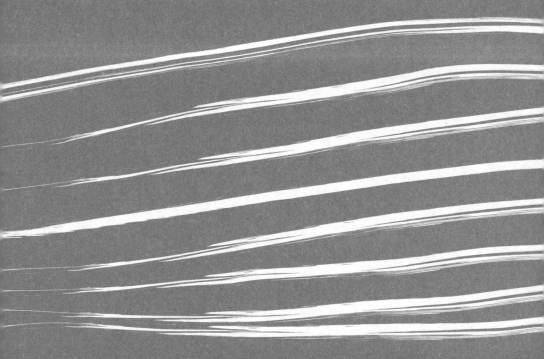

"I have learned that the roller coaster of my
emotions isn't a good indicator of the health
of our marriage. What works is treating our
marriage as our most precious possession
and investing time in it."

— Miles Protter

Plan a date together

	Mon	Tues	Wed	Thurs	Fri	Sat	Sun
☀ Morning							
☁ Afternoon							
🌙 Evening							

My turn / your turn to organize what we do.

This week, we could..

Conversation starter on your next date:
If money was no object in planning a memorable date for us,
I would...

You make me feel loved when you...

> A healthy marriage involves an equal
> partnership within which we work out,
> and then both work to, our strengths.

Making decisions

In the left-hand column, write down who decided what in your parents' (or main caregivers') marriage as a percentage of their influence (e.g., 50:50 or 70:30 or 90:10). Then in the right-hand column put your expectations for your own marriage.

Discuss what you have each put. (If you grew up with one parent, only fill in the right-hand column.)

My parents		Decisions	Our marriage	
Father	Mother		Husband	Wife
		Choice of new car		
		Choice of where to live		
		Choice of furniture		
		Choice of china		
		Choice of own clothes		
		Choice of vacations		
		Choice of decoration of home		
		Choice of pictures		
		Choice of how to bring up children		
		Choice of TV shows		
		Choice of food		
		Choice of number of children		
		Choice of husband's job		
		Choice of wife's job		
		Determining how money is spent		

Connection

RECAP

– Ask your partner what they found most helpful in Session 3 for your relationship.

Session 4 – Connection

> How do we keep our love alive and stay connected over the whole course of a marriage?

Spend time together

Keeping love alive is a deliberate choice. It involves:

- being intentional

- investing in our friendship

- making a daily habit of connecting with each other

Benefits of a weekly date:

- regular opportunity for effective communication

- keeps the romance, love, fun, and friendship alive in our marriage

> When we put our screens away and focus our attention on our partner, we're communicating powerfully, "I value you above anyone else."

Tips for planning regular dates:

Try to plan at least two hours every week to do something together you both enjoy

- plan ahead (put them in your calendars for the next 3 months)

- make them different and special, whether you stay in or go out

Make them a priority over other demands

- protect this time from interruptions (friends, family, phone)

Be creative; vary what you do (time and place)

- don't set the bar too high (a date doesn't have to be expensive)

Make use of mealtimes

- put away screens

- make conversation—ask questions your partner will enjoy answering

CONVERSATION 1

10 minutes

BUILDING YOUR FRIENDSHIP

Write a list of six things you enjoy doing together.

1.

2.

3.

4.

5.

6.

Compare what you have written. How could you make sure you are still doing these things together five / ten / fifteen years into marriage?

Discovering your partner's needs

Discovering what makes our partner feel loved builds deeper connection between us and keeps our love growing.

We can be very different to each other in the ways we give and receive love.

The five love languages[1]

1. Loving words

2. Thoughtful presents

3. Physical affection

4. Quality time

5. Kind actions

All five ways of expressing love are important in every marriage, but often there will be one or two of them that communicate love in the way we particularly understand it.

Often our partner's love language will be different to ours

- learning to show them love effectively can be like learning a different language

- it takes effort, discipline, and practice

[1] The teaching on the Five Love Languages is adapted from Dr. Gary Chapman's bestselling book, *The 5 Love Languages®: The Secret to Love That Lasts* (© 2015). Published by Northfield Publishing. Used by permission.

CONVERSATION 2

15 minutes

DISCOVERING YOUR LOVE LANGUAGES

Write down six specific occasions on which you have particularly known your partner's love for you.

I have known your love for me when:

1.

2.

3.

4.

5.

6.

Taking into consideration the six examples above, try to put the five ways of showing love in order of importance for you. Then consider which order you would put them in for your partner. When you have both finished, show each other what you have put.

For you Number 1–5 (1 = most important)	Love expressed through:	For your partner Number 1–5 (1 = most important)
	Words	
	Time	
	Presents	
	Touch	
	Actions	

If necessary, correct the column "For your partner" if their answers reveal a different order.

Go online to **www.5lovelanguages.com** to fill in a short questionnaire to confirm the order of importance of these love languages for you.

Building your sexual relationship

Sex joins us together, not just physically, but emotionally, psychologically, and even spiritually.

> Think of your sexual relationship as a journey of discovery over a lifetime.

Good sex is **us-focused**, not me-focused.

How to establish and maintain a pattern of good sex in marriage:

1. Get your hearts in sync

Be ready to talk

- can be difficult as deeply private and requires vulnerability
- tell each other what turns you on and what turns you off
- don't leave it to guesswork

Bring closure to past sexual relationships.

- past relationships can cause jealousy and mistrust
- be honest with each other
- if necessary, disconnect on social media from people you were once attracted to and delete emails / texts / photos
- may need to say sorry to and forgive each other

2. Get your heads straight

Good sex has so much to do with our state of mind

- fill your minds with what is beautiful, honorable, and mutually respectful about sex
- talk about expectations and any fears

Problems resulting from abuse or other sexual trauma from the past may require professional help (ask your course leader for advice)

- If you are struggling in your sexual relationship, don't bury the problem

> **Most sexual problems are common and solvable.**

- talk together
- read a book on sex together (see Appendix 6 for recommended books)
- seek expert help if necessary

Using pornography has a damaging effect psychologically and will impact a couple's sexual relationship negatively. If pornography is an issue in your relationship, have an honest and non-judgmental conversation with your partner. Taking steps to change your habits will have a hugely positive impact on your relationship and will make having good sex a reality in marriage.

Low self esteem and poor body image affect our sexual responses

- build your partner's confidence
- keep admiring each other's body

> **Sex affects every other part of our marriage relationship and every other part of our marriage affects our sexual intimacy.**

TALKING ABOUT SEX (PART 1)

Complete whichever of the following sentences apply to you and your relationship.
Then discuss what you have written with your partner.

Getting your hearts in sync

I am anxious about…

For example: *expectations about sex / feeling vulnerable in talking about sex /
a past sexual relationship / family planning / being seen naked*

Getting your head straight

My thinking about sex has been affected by…

For example: *my upbringing / unhelpful messages about sex from… / trauma from the
past / low self-esteem / pornography*

3. Get your bodies set

Significant differences between men and women in sexual arousal

- give time for preparation and arousal

Create a climate of trust

- good sex is dependent on allowing other
  parts of our relationship to develop

- strong connection between giving
  ourselves to each other in our marriage
  vows and in our sexual relationship

- practice self-control

> **Sex is about the giving of
> our bodies to each other.**

Four practical tips

1. Plan for sex on a regular basis
- enough to stay closely connected
- be intentional
- make it a priority

2. Make your bedroom special
- make it a space that feels relaxed and safe
- leave phones and screens outside the bedroom

3. Be creative
- talk about what you like or might like together
- avoid getting stuck in a rut
- be imaginative, gentle, and respectful of each other

4. Plan times away alone together
- go away occasionally to a different location

CONVERSATION 4

10 minutes

TALKING ABOUT SEX (PART 2)

Complete the following sentence. Then discuss what you have written with your partner.

Getting your body set

I would like us to talk about...

For example: *the different ways we are aroused / keeping sex for marriage / the regularity of sex / our bedroom / being creative in lovemaking*

"Do not arouse or awaken love until it so desires."

— SONG OF SOLOMON 2:7; 3:5; 8:4

Continuing the Conversation

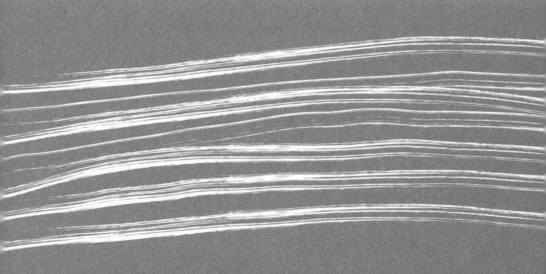

"Romance is the bridge between the everyday world of practicality and the private place of our sexual relationship."

— Nicky and Sila Lee

Plan a date together

	Mon	Tues	Wed	Thurs	Fri	Sat	Sun
☼ Morning							
☁ Afternoon							
☾ Evening							

My turn / your turn to organize what we do.

This week, we could...

> **Conversation starter on your next date:**
>
> Ask each other, "How much time do you like to spend with others during the week and how much time when it's just the two of us?"
>
> Ask each other, "What does your ideal weekend look like?"

Time apart

Every marriage needs a balance of time together and time apart.

There are two dangers:

    1. Too much time apart

    2. No space to pursue separate interests

Each write down any individual interests you expect to pursue without your partner:

    1.

    2.

    3.

How frequently and how much time would these take?

    1.

    2.

    3.

Write down any individual interests you expect your partner to pursue without you:

    1.

    2.

    3.

How frequently and how much time might these take?

    1.

    2.

    3.

Now compare and discuss your answers.

Adventure

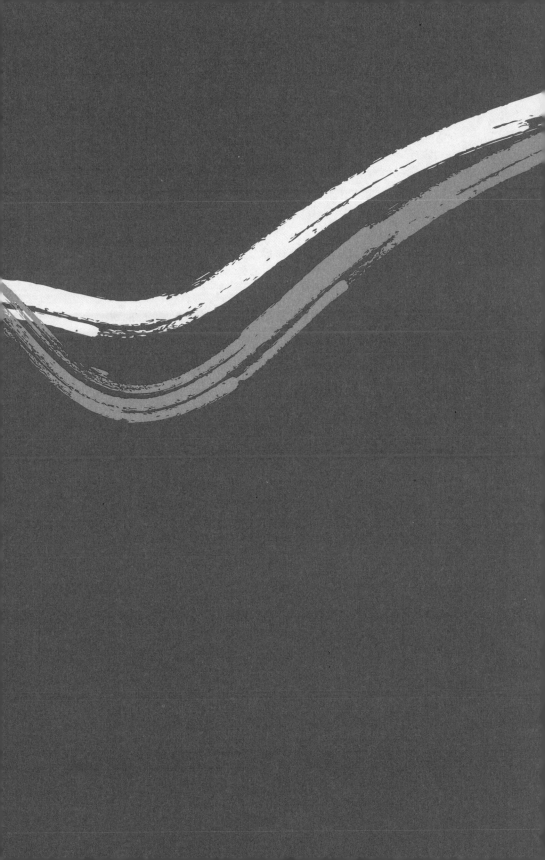

Session 5 – Adventure

Marriage provides us with one of life's greatest opportunities·and one of its greatest challenges:

- **the opportunity** to build the most intimate of relationships, the benefits of which go way beyond ourselves
- **the challenge** to go on learning what it means to love another person, to look beyond our own needs and to go on finding out what is important to our partner, and then make adjustments in our own behavior

Are there ways that I need to change for the sake of our partnership?

Pulling in harmony

1. Show appreciation

No marriage can survive a lack of appreciation.

Express your appreciation of each other even when you don't feel like it.

Showing appreciation every day will draw out your partner's potential and build their self-esteem.

"

For every one critical remark, there needs to be at least five positive ones.

DR. JOHN GOTTMAN

CONVERSATION 1

10 minutes

EXPRESSING APPRECIATION

Write a list of your partner's strengths and the qualities you most admire in him or her:

1.

2.

3.

4.

5.

6.

Then take turns to read out to your partner what you have each put.

The more we express gratitude TO each other, the more grateful we become FOR each other.

2. Let go of unrealistic expectations

Marriage cannot meet all of our needs.

Our partner will never love us perfectly.

We have to accept our partner as they are rather than as we would like them to be.

Unrealistic expectations lead to a downward spiral of demands, disappointment, blame, and criticism.

If we expect perfection, we'll never be satisfied.

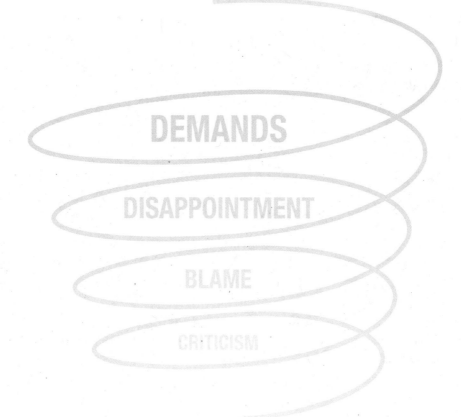

DEMANDS

DISAPPOINTMENT

BLAME

CRITICISM

3. Be prepared to change

We can change ourselves; we can't change our partner.

Find out what matters to your partner.

> Showing our partner in big ways and small ways that we're prepared to change our behavior, rather than trying to force them to change, sends a powerful message of love.

4. Recognize our common overreactions

We may overreact when our partner touches a "raw spot"

- this will usually be a result of negative experiences from our past

- may cause us to charge (like the rhino) or withdraw (like the hedgehog)

We need to look at our reactions and ask:

- "Is that reasonable?"

- "Is that in proportion to the situation?"

Change is possible but usually happens gradually:

- it takes courage

- requires self-awareness

- involves being vulnerable and talking about why we react as we do

- may involve forgiving those who have hurt us or let us down in the past

CONVERSATION 2

15 minutes

REFLECTING ON YOUR UPBRINGING

1. Describe to your partner any situations in which you know you overreact.

For example: "*I get angry and moody when I am being rushed to get ready.*"

2. Explain any reasons you are aware of for this overreaction.

For example: "*This reminds me of how my dad used to rush us out of the door for school in the mornings and shout at me to hurry up. I always felt unprepared for my day and annoyed with him.*"

3. Reflect on whether there is anyone you need to forgive from your past.

For example: "*I need to forgive my dad for getting so angry and impatient with me every morning.*"

4. Tell your partner how they could help you to avoid this overreaction in your relationship.

For example: "*Always give me plenty of time to get ready and try to avoid shouting at me if we are behind schedule.*"

Now show each other what you have put and discuss how you can help each other.

Agree on our priorities

Our priorities in life will be determined by our values.

We may have very different personalities, but having similar core values and an agreed set of priorities will enable a couple to build a strong marriage.

Share your dreams, aspirations, hopes, and longings

  - set aside time to work out an order of priority for different areas of your lives

> Giving priority to the people and the values that matter most to us doesn't just happen—we have to be intentional about it.

Four areas that will be affected by our priorities:

1. Friendships

  - don't cut yourselves off as a couple

  - protect your marriage from any relationships that might threaten it

  - set boundaries to guard yourselves from the risk of an affair

2. Children and family life

  - discuss your expectations for having children

  - keep making time for each other

3. Work

  - don't compete with each other

  - talk about how you would balance work and taking care of children

4. Spirituality

- exploring our core beliefs can draw us closer together

- talk about what beliefs and values you would want to pass on to children

- praying together connects us with each other as well as with God

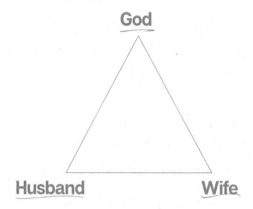

As we each look to God to receive and experience his love, forgiveness, and a sense of his purpose for our lives, we are better able to love each other.

Supporting each other

Consider praying together for each other

- daily prayer—ask your partner: "What can I pray for you today?"

- focus on each other's needs

- accept the same requests day after day

- start with thankfulness

- praying doesn't just happen—needs to be planned

If you don't pray, ask your partner: "How can I best support you today?"

A cord of three strands is not quickly broken.

— ECCLESIASTES 4:12

CONVERSATION 3

10 minutes

WORKING OUT YOUR PRIORITIES

Try to write a list of your top five priorities as a couple.

Then put against each priority one way you would hope to live that out in your lives together.

Use the list of examples below to help you, but do not be limited by it. When you have finished, compare and discuss what you have each put.

Examples of values: *health, creativity, marriage relationship, sport, vocation / job, good stewardship of money and possessions, local community involvement, adventure, having fun, hospitality, friendships, care of environment, nurturing children, ongoing education, spirituality / relationship with God, wider family, generosity, church activities.*

Examples of how you might plan to live out a value:
Relationship with God: seek to pray together for each other each day.
Our marriage relationship: set aside time each week to have fun together.

Priority	How to live that value out
1.	:
2.	:
3.	:
4.	:
5.	:

Adventurers and nurturers

Recognize whether one of you is more "adventuring" and the other more "nurturing".

> **Every marriage needs to give enough space for both adventuring and nurturing. When you can get these two forces working well in your marriage, marriage itself becomes one of life's great adventures.**

Adventurers

Tend to want to make the most of all the possibilities that life offers.

View marriage itself as a joint adventure.

Nurturers

Often see their marriage as a safe place to return to after whatever adventures or challenges life brings.

Nurturers bring consistency and routine in the relationship.

There is no gender correlation to either style.

Both adventuring and nurturing make an equally important contribution to the relationship

    – too little adventure and your relationship can become stagnated

    – too much adventure and you can be overstretched

As a couple, your responsibility is to value both the energy of adventure and the security of recovery.

> **"**
>
> **Everybody is looking for two things in life: adventure and security.**
> G. K. CHESTERTON

CONVERSATION 4

10 minutes

ADVENTURER OR NURTURER

Complete the following exercise on your own and then talk about it together.

Mark with your initials where you think you and your partner each come on the line between the two extremes:

ADVENTURER   **NURTURER**

ADVENTURER	NURTURER
New friends	Same friends
Explore new places	Create a secure home
Enjoy change	Enjoy routine
Love traveling	Love staying put
Holiday in new places	Return to same places
Relax by being active	Relax by being restful
Like uncertainty	Like certainty
Like surprises	Don't like surprises
Enjoy a challenge	Prefer comfort zone
Like flexible working hours	Prefer set working hours
Energetic	Relaxed
Pursue new interests	Prefer familiar interests
Enjoy setting off	Enjoy returning home
Live on adrenaline	Live more calmly
Need enough action	Need enough sleep
Take risks	Risk-averse
More task-oriented	More relational
Always wanting to try something new	Enjoy sticking to known tasks

– Discuss whether one of you is more on the adventuring side and the other more on the nurturing side.

– Discuss whether you need to increase the adventuring or the nurturing in your relationship.

– Talk about how well you balance each other out.

When we apply the tools in this course—talking and listening well, using each other's love languages, expressing our appreciation for each other, living out our shared priorities—we build a relationship of love that can weather even the strongest storm.

Place me like a seal over your heart, like a seal on your arm; for love is as strong as death, its jealousy unyielding as the grave. It burns like blazing fire, like a mighty flame. Many waters cannot quench love; rivers cannot sweep it away. If one were to give all the wealth of one's house for love, it would be utterly scorned.
— SONG OF SOLOMON 8:6-7

Continuing the Conversation

"Over the whole lifetime of a marriage we
will never fully know everything about our
partner—there will always be more to discover
and appreciate."

— Nicky and Sila Lee

Plan a date together

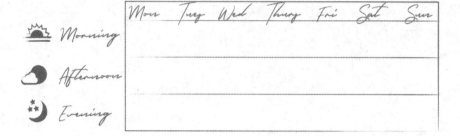

	Mon	Tues	Wed	Thurs	Fri	Sat	Sun
☀ Morning							
☁ Afternoon							
☾ Evening							

My turn / your turn to organize what we do.

This week, we could...

Ideas for our dates this month...

1.

2.

3.

4.

Conversation starter on your next date:
Tell your partner, "If I think about us in twenty years' time, the thing I most look forward to is..."

The three things I most admire about you are...

Putting it into practice

Three things I especially want to remember and practice from The Pre-Marriage Course:

1.

2.

3.

Show your partner what you have written.

Now ask him / her, "What three things would you especially like me to remember and practice from the course?" Write them down here:

1.

2.

3.

Appendix 1

Ready for marriage?

(see *The Marriage Book*, Appendix 1)

- The sharing test

Do I want to share the rest of my life with my partner?

- The character test

Do I regard my partner as being kind?

- The strength test

Does our love give me energy and strength, or does it drain me?

- The respect test

Do I respect my partner?

- The habit test

Do I accept my partner as they are now (bad habits and all)?

- The quarrel test

Are we able to admit our mistakes, apologize, and forgive each other?

- The interest test

Do we have interests in common as a foundation for friendship?

- The time test

Have we weathered all the seasons and a variety of situations together?

These tests have been adapted from *I Married You* by Walter Trobisch (IVP, 1973).

If you are unable to answer yes to the questions above, we suggest you discuss your feelings with someone other than your partner.

Appendix 2

Ephesians 5:21–33

21Submit to one another out of reverence for Christ. 22Wives, submit yourselves to your own husbands as you do to the Lord. 23For the husband is the head of the wife as Christ is the head of the church, his body, of which he is the Saviour. 24Now as the church submits to Christ, so also wives should submit to their husbands in everything. 25Husbands, love your wives, just as Christ loved the church and gave himself up for her 26to make her holy, cleansing her by the washing with water through the word, 27and to present her to himself as a radiant church, without stain or wrinkle or any other blemish, but holy and blameless. 28In this same way, husbands ought to love their wives as their own bodies. He who loves his wife loves himself. 29After all, no one ever hated their own body, but they feed and care for their body, just as Christ does the church—30for we are members of his body. 31"For this reason a man will leave his father and mother and be united to his wife, and the two will become one flesh." 32This is a profound mystery—but I am talking about Christ and the church. 33However, each one of you also must love his wife as he loves himself, and the wife must respect her husband.

1. The context of the whole passage is: "Submit to one another out of reverence for Christ" (Ephesians 5:21). (Submitting is the opposite of lording it over or seeking to control another. Marriage is designed to be a relationship of mutual giving as we seek to serve each other and to put each other's needs ahead of our own.)

2. Compare the duties of husband and wife (more is written to the husband owing to the prevailing culture in which a husband had total rights over his household):

   - the husband's duty: "Husbands, love your wives, just as Christ loved the church and gave himself up for her... husbands ought to love their wives as their own bodies." (Ephesians 5:25,28)

   - the wife's duty: "Wives, submit yourselves to your own husbands as you do to the Lord" (Ephesians 5:22)

3. "Head" does not necessarily mean leader. St. Paul could be emphasizing the close connection between husband and wife in marriage. They cannot act independently of each other any longer.

4. Servant-leadership means taking responsibility rather than leaving the issue to our husband or wife: we should take the initiative rather than taking control.

5. The whole passage is set in the context of seeking God's will rather than seeking to impose our own will: "Find out what pleases the Lord... understand what the Lord's will is" (Ephesians 5:10,17).

Appendix 3

The marriage vows

The priest/minister says to the bridegroom:

[Name], will you take [Name] to be your wife? Will you love her, comfort her, honor and protect her, and, forsaking all others, be faithful to her as long as you both shall live?

He answers: I will.

The priest/minister says to the bride:

[Name], will you take [Name] to be your husband? Will you love him, comfort him, honor and protect him, and, forsaking all others, be faithful to him as long as you both shall live?

She answers: I will.

The bridegroom takes the bride's right hand in his, and says:

I, [Name], take you, [Name], to be my wife, to have and to hold from this day forward, for better, for worse, for richer, for poorer, in sickness and in health, to love and to cherish, till death us do part, according to God's holy law, and this is my solemn vow.

The bride takes the bridegroom's right hand in hers, and says:

I, [Name], take you, [Name], to be my husband, to have and to hold from this day forward, for better, for worse, for richer, for poorer, in sickness and in health, to love and to cherish, till death us do part, according to God's holy law, and this is my solemn vow.

The bridegroom places the ring on the fourth finger of the bride's left hand and, holding it there, says:

[Name], I give you this ring as a sign of our marriage. With my body I honor you, all that I am I give to you, and all that I have I share with you, within the love of God, Father, Son, and Holy Spirit.

The bride places a ring on the fourth finger of the bridegroom's left hand and, holding it there, says:

[Name], I give you this ring (or, if only one ring is used: I receive this ring) as a sign of our marriage. With my body I honor you, all that I am I give to you, and all that I have I share with you, within the love of God, Father, Son, and Holy Spirit.

Appendix 4

Creating a budget

(see also *The Marriage Book*, Appendix 3: "Working out a budget")

Money management tips from CAP:

Create a budget

Agree on a budget together—and stick to it. It might sound simple, but this is the easiest way to keep track of how much money you have and exactly what you're spending it on.

Save, save, save!

Even if you can only afford to save a small amount each month, eventually it all adds up. Having a savings pot you can dip into when facing unexpected costs could be a lifesaver. What about planning ahead for specific things like Christmas or vacations?

Do your research

If you've been with the same energy supplier for over a year, the chances are you're paying more than you need to. By researching the different options available, you can find the cheapest deal that suits your individual needs.

Pay with cash

Pay with cash instead of card. By handing over physical money, you can stay aware of what you're buying. This also means that when the money's gone, it's gone, which might make you think twice about that thing you "really need".

If you want to find out more about Christians Against Poverty, visit us at capuk.org.
To book on to a CAP Money Course in your area visit **capmoneycourse.org**.

Monthly Budget Planner

Average monthly income (work out annual amount)

Joint salaries $..............

Other sources of income $..............

Total (1) $....................... ÷ 12 $..............
(monthly)

Fixed regular expenditure (work out annual amount)	Actual	Budget
Rent/mortgage	$..........	$..........
Tax	$..........	$..........
Utilities (gas, electricity, water)	$..........	$..........
Insurance	$..........	$..........
Loan repayment	$..........	$..........
Travel	$..........	$..........
Car – tax, insurance	$..........	$..........
Charitable giving	$..........	$..........
Other	$..........	$..........
Total (2) $....................... ÷ 12	$..........	$..........
	(monthly)	(monthly)

Flexible "essential" expenditure (estimate annual amount)	Actual	Budget
Household (food, pharmacy, etc.)	$..........	$..........
Clothes / shoes	$..........	$..........
Car maintenance	$..........	$..........
Telephone	$..........	$..........
Other	$..........	$..........
Total (3) $....................... ÷ 12	$..........	$..........
	(monthly)	(monthly)

Flexible "non-essential" expenditure (estimate annual amount)	Actual	Budget
Entertainment / hospitality	$..........	$..........
Presents	$..........	$..........
Sport / leisure	$..........	$..........
Vacations	$..........	$..........
Eating out	$..........	$..........
Other	$..........	$..........
Total (4) $....................... ÷ 12	$..........	$..........
	(monthly)	(monthly)

	Actual	Budget
Monthly sum for savings/emergencies **Total (5)**	$..........	$..........
Add together total monthly expenditure **(2, 3, 4, 5)**	$..........	$..........
Compare to total monthly income (1)	$..........	$..........

Appendix 5

Suggested readings for a marriage service

Psalms 19; 84; 85; 91; 121; 139:1–18

Ecclesiastes 4:9–12

Song of Solomon 2:10–13; 8:6–7

Isaiah 40:25–31

John 2:1–11

John 15:1–4, 9–17

1 Corinthians 13:1–8(a)

Ephesians 3:14–21

Ephesians 5:21–33

Philippians 2:1–11

Philippians 4:4–9

Colossians 3:12–17

1 John 4:7–16

Appendix 6

Recommended books

The Five Love Languages by Gary Chapman (Moody Press, Northfield Publishing, 2015)

The Other Side of Love: Handling Anger in a Godly Way by Gary Chapman (Moody Press, Northfield Publishing, 1999)

Boundaries in Marriage by Dr. Henry Cloud and Dr. John Townsend (Zondervan, 2002)

Rules of Engagement: How to Plan a Successful Wedding/How to Build a Marriage that Lasts by Richard and Katharine Hill (Lion Hudson Plc, 2009)

Created for Connection by Dr. Sue Johnson with Kenneth Sanderfer (Little, Brown US, 2016)

The Meaning of Marriage by Timothy Keller with Kathy Keller (Hodder & Stoughton, 2011)

The Marriage Book by Nicky and Sila Lee (Alpha International, 2009)

The Mystery of Marriage by Mike Mason (Multnomah, 2005)

Loving Against the Odds by Rob Parsons (Hodder & Stoughton, 2010)

The Sixty Minute Marriage by Rob Parsons (Hodder & Stoughton, 2009)

A Celebration of Sex by Douglas Rosenau (Thomas Nelson, 2002)

Seasons of Sex & Intimacy by Emma Waring (Hullo Creative, 2018)

To purchase DVDs and study journals for The Marriage Course and The Pre-Marriage Course, visit **churchsource.com/collections/alpha-marriage**, or pay for digital access. For the first time ever, all the talks will be available to purchase online; while access to the updated training videos, introductory videos and downloadable Leaders' Guides will be available at no charge at **alphausa.org/marriage**.

If you are interested in finding out more about the Christian faith and would like to be put in touch with your nearest Alpha, visit **www.alphausa.org**

Follow us on social media @marriagecourses